ClickBank Money Machine

Make Money Online With ClickBank Affiliate Marketing

by Lance MacNeil

Copyright © dsk-enterprise Inc. Ltd. 2014
All rights reserved. No part of this publication may be reproduced in any form without written consent of the author and the publisher. The information contained in this book may not be stored in a retrieval system, or transmitted in any form by any means, electronic, mechanical, photocopying or otherwise without the written permission of the publisher. This book may not be resold, hired out or otherwise disposed by way of trade in any form of binding or cover other than that in which it is published, without the written consent of the publisher.

Legal Disclaimer

The information contained in this book is strictly for educational purpose only. The content of this book is the sole expression and opinion of its author, and not necessarily that of the publisher. It is not intended to cure, treat, and diagnose any kind of disease or medical condition. It is sold with the understanding that the publisher is not rendering any type of medical, psychological, legal, or any other kind of professional advice. You should seek the services of a competent professional before applying concepts in this book. Neither the publisher nor the individual author(s) shall be liable for any physical, psychological, emotional, financial, or commercial damages, directly or indirectly by the use of this material, which is provided "as is", and without warranties. Therefore, if you wish to apply ideas contained in this book, you are taking full responsibility for your actions

Table of Contents

1: What is ClickBank?
2: How to Make Money with ClikBank
3: Understanding Gravity and Hoplinks
4: Best ways to promote ClickBank
5: How to Succeed as an Affiliate
6: How to become a Vendor
7: Dos and Don'ts for a Vendor
8: Why you should be at ClickBank
9: 10 Things to know about ClickBank
10: ClickBank is not a Scam
Conclusion

Introduction

Have you ever tried to find a way to make money online? If we type in "How To Make Money Online" in the google search engine, there are 2.4 million websites with the related keywords.

These websites all claim how you can make a boat load of money if you send them $49.00 and follow simple instructions. Through my experience with making money online, most of these websites are scams. The reason why these scammers continue to prey on the internet is because they are making money.

You might ask, "If they're a scam, then how come they are making money? Good question! The answer is what you call "Law of Averages". You see, throughout history the return rate for purchases made through the internet is less than 10%! Did you get that? That's right, less than 10%.

For some unknown reason, many people find it a hassle to return things they do not wish to keep. They would rather lose their hard earned money then to ask for a refund. Since they were duped into buying the money making scam in the first place, they feel as though they legitimately deserve to lose their money. I can't figure this out, but these are the facts.

There are some legitimate ways to make money online, and one of them is ClickBank. Do you know anything about "ClickBank"?

ClickBank is the largest online marketplace where digital products are sold. It has the largest affiliate network on the web today. So, if you are looking to make the most out of the benefits offered by this amazing platform, this book will serve you a lot of purpose as it uncovers all the things you need to know about ClickBank affiliate marketing.

1: What is ClickBank?

ClickBank is a privately owned company located in Boise, Idaho. In a very short time period, ClickBank has become a global leader in the digital market.

Clickbank was founded in 1998 by Tim and Eileen Barber, as a subsidiary of Keynetics. In 2011, Revenue Magazine named ClickBank as the largest market with the most affiliate network in the USA.

By this time, ClickBank has more than 100,000 affiliate marketers. In the same year, this company claimed to have paid a whopping $1.8 billion to its vendors and affiliates, processed over 35,000 transactions per day, and generated $350 million as its annual revenue.

They have over 50,000 products to choose from in various categories. It provides services to more than 200 countries around the world. These wide ranges of products in so many countries have made ClickBank one of the most popular sites on the internet. Its popularity had traveled far and wide, and it catered to a very diverse range of audience, and consumers.

ClickBank has consistently been rated as one of the most visited websites online. The shopping experiences offered by ClickBank to its customers are safe and efficient. All the products provided by ClickBank are backed by their 60 day 100% money back guarantee.

Its main purpose is to serve as a link or a connection between digital content creators, who are also known as "Vendors", and the promoters who are also known as "Affiliate Marketers".

The affiliate marketers promote the products to prospective customers. Their main job is to make the products sell through their marketing techniques. Their job is very similar to the people working in the marketing and advertising industry. They make the products look attractive to the prospective consumers, let them be aware of the product, and if they buy through your ad or link, you will earn a commission.

These affiliate marketers are the back bone of this industry, as it is through them the products reaches the public. However, to create your own digital product most vendors have to go through a tedious task that include product creation, website creation, web sales copy, processing orders, customer support, financial management, and other technical issues.

You can hire a professional to perform all these services if you have the financial means. All these services are very challenging and complicated and involve a lot of coordination and development of complex systems.

By being an affiliate marketer, you just have to spread the word about the 'product and the vendor' and your job is done.

This can be done by developing contacts over the web, joining social media, creating a blog, email marketing, writing reviews, and a lot of other techniques. Most of the consumers do not have the knowledge of the products available online. This is where your job as an affiliate marketer comes to place.

An affiliate marketer is given a special link through which the customer connects to the sales page and introduces you as the authentic marketer of the product, in which you will receive a commission if the sales are made through the affiliate link.

Many such affiliate programs are available online but ClickBank remains at the top in internet marketing and sales. They have the distinction of being the world's largest provider of digital products and services, which comprise mainly of software and eBooks.

All these details about ClickBank have probably made you think that it must be quite difficult to become an affiliate. On the contrary, it is quite simple; a single user registration to ClickBank makes you an affiliate.

Experts have found that the average price of Clickbank products is about $40 and the average commission rate is about 50%. However, there are some top sellers who offer up to 75% commission. This rate of commission is very high and rewarding. For this all you have to do is to:

- Open account with ClickBank
- Find a product or service that interest you.
- Obtain hoplink for the product you are promoting
- Promote product using your new affiliate link
- Make a sale and you earn a commission
- Repeat the process
- That's all there is to it!

It is quite easy once you get the hang of it, although there is a learning curve just like any other money making opportunities. Good thing about this program is you don't have to quit your job to be an affiliate marketer. It takes less than an hour to get the word out through social media, emails, and messages. You just have to wait for the contacts to turn into sales.

The vast world of internet is continuously flooded with different marketing opportunities that aim to help people achieve their financial goals. ClickBank affiliate marketing is consistently producing a lot of buzz inside the marketing world.

2: How to Make Money with ClickBank

As more and more people are trying to find ways to make money online, ClickBank affiliate marketing opportunities keeps popping up. With ClickBank, everyone is given the chance to make money as long as they know what they are doing. Are you interested in making money with ClickBank? If you are, please continue reading.

The Breakdown of Profit Generation Process with ClickBank

One of the easiest ways to make money with ClickBank is through selling the newest and the most popular products. Once you open an account with ClickBank, you will be given a ClickBank ID. Here are the 7 steps you need to become an affiliate marketer.

Step 1:

Go to ClickBank.com and open your free account.

Step 2:

Visit the ClickBank Marketplace and then choose your niche in the Category List. Select a niche that you have some knowledge or interest in, or something you are passionate about. After you have chosen your selection, look through other products in similar category and choose 2 other products to market.

Try choosing products with the gravity score of 20 and above. It is recommended that you only promote products guaranteed to provide genuine value. If you offer good product, surely people will trust your advice and opinion, eventually leading to more sales.

Step 3:

Perform keyword search for every product that you select. You can use the free keyword search tool from google called "google keyword planner"

Step 4:

Create at least 2 articles that tackle each of the three products. This is why it's a great idea to choose products from similar category. You may duplicate common statements regarding the category itself to save time in writing. However, make sure not to overuse such method. At least strive to have 90 percent original content in every article.

For every product you have chosen, you may make one of the articles in the review format. Normally, a product review starts by producing a statement to display that you are an avid reviewer. Then, it comes down to describing the features of the product. Ultimately, you will recommend the product with your approval stamp, while showing the many benefits and value to your readers.

Step 5:

Post the articles to some free directories. Get the ads indexed in popular search engines. You will be able to perform this manually through keying in the query box search engine "get indexed". Or alternatively, you may do this using the automatic submission software.

Stay with the trial version or free version for an economical option. In order to find free programs, type "free submission software" or "free article submission software" in your favorite search engine query box.

Step 6:

Wait until your articles have been indexed within the search engines and then have them submitted to different article directory websites. There are many article directories in the internet, but only submit it to the most popular ones.

Step 7:

Follow these steps mentioned above and are ready to make money with ClickBank, as you promote different products.

3: Understanding Gravity and Hoplinks

What is ClickBank Gravity?

Gravity is used to factor in the number of affiliates who earned a commission by promoting the vendor's products during the past 12 weeks. If the gravity is higher, more affiliates are earning commissions from such product at this point of time.

Based on ClickBank's definition of Gravity, it is a performance statistic, which is a number that displays a distinctive calculation through ClickBank. The calculation considers the number of various affiliates who received a commission by marketing the product for more than the previous twelve weeks.

While newer transactions are provided with a higher value, such number could offer you the idea of the latest products, when it comes to being marketed by several affiliates. On the other hand, high level of gravity may also mean that there will be lots of competition in marketing the same product.

Calculation Process of ClickBank Gravity

ClickBank measures the amount of gravity through the use of weighted sum method. In this calculation, ClickBank adds between 1.0 and 0.1 to the total gravity for each affiliate who produced a sales in the past 12 weeks. ClickBank identifies a specific amount in the range. However, the newer affiliate sales are provided with a higher gravity.

The value amount of gravity begins at zero and normally ranges between 0 and 800. A product having a zero gravity means that no affiliates have produced any sales in the past twelve weeks. On the other hand, a product having a 300 gravity level means there are probably hundreds of affiliates promoting the same product and earned a commission within the previous twelve weeks.

ClickBank utilizes the amount of gravity as a facet of the overall "productivity level" of the products when ranking them within the ClickBank marketplace.

Understanding the Use of Hoplinks

To become a successful ClickBank affiliate, it is important for you to understand the proper use of hoplinks, which is a tracking URL to market ClickBank products online.

A Hoplink is a recommendation monitoring URL. It is simply a site address, such as www.Google.com or www.Yahoo.com. On the other hand, these URLs for referral tracking are special, as they route web traffic using the ClickBank Hoplink Monitoring System.

Every hoplinks takes in custom information, which is directing users who click on the URL to the website of ClickBank vendor by which they will hopefully create a purchase.

In addition, a hoplink acquires information about the person who does the visit, who is you, the ClickBank affiliate. This makes sure that when a user clicks on the hoplink, and results in a purchasing of the product, you will be credited for the sale.

How Do You Create Hoplinks?

There are 2 primary ways on how you can make customized hoplinks, which you may use to market ClickBank products. One of them and the most ordinary way is through automatically producing hoplinks by the use of ClickBank marketplace. You may search through the category section and find the product you want to promote, and then hit the button saying "Promote", which is located on the product listing's right side. Such hoplink would automatically be encrypted through the use of Hoplink Shield to gain additional security. After you have created the Hoplink, you should copy the address and then paste it in any place you wish to have the product promoted.

Prior to starting the promotion, it is recommended that you have the Hoplink pasted into your computer's text file through your Notepad or Microsoft Word, and then have the file saved. This should allow you to monitor all the varied hoplinks you have created.

An alternate way to create hoplinks is knowing your account nickname from ClickBank along with vendor's nickname you like to promote. Once you know these two nicknames, then you can make your very own hoplink through directing people to the website address with this particular format: http://clickbankID.vendorID.hop.ClickBank.net.

To allow the hoplink to work, all you need to do is to replace the "ClickbankID" using your nickname and "VendorID" using the ClickBank nickname of the vendor. Now that you understand how gravity and hoplink work, we'll move on to the next chapter.

4: Best ways to Promote ClickBank

ClickBank is the premier affiliate program for most people who are new to online marketing. So what is the best way to promote ClickBank? This may be one of the questions may you have. Well, there are several effective ways to do it.

Use an Article Marketing Technique

One of the best ways to advertise ClickBank involves the use of an article promotion technique. The first step is to write engaging, well-written and informative articles. When you visit a number of article submission directories, you will find that most of them come with a resource box that allows anyone to place links to the landing pages.

What are landing pages? These are the pages on websites that market a certain service or product. The content of a great article must concentrate on offering helpful recommendations and advice associated with the product.

In other words, your article should offer useful, helpful advice. For example: If a ClickBank product is associated with SEO then you should provide some useful suggestions and tips inside the article. You should include in your article some information about SEO and how it works.

You may explain what Search Engine Optimization is and the steps to best optimize a website. You need to provide what's useful but leave your readers craving for more. This is the outcome that you should aim for when you start to promote ClickBank products.

Do not forget that your resource box must attract the readers to click on the landing page of the ClickBank product you are promoting. This is the most efficient way to attain SEO and persuade the readers that the ClickBank product you offer can be extremely beneficial them.

Please take note that your article marketing tactic must always include "giving" instead of "selling" as nobody wants to get a sales pitch. People who use the web today are much smarter as they can easily distinguish if a certain article is a good source of information or not.

People today look for readily available details and the affiliate marketer must struggle to become an expert on ClickBank through appropriate research in order to provide the needed information.

It is the only time when you will be able to gain the trust of your reader. Learning how to write great articles and practicing proper research are proven to be among the best ways to market ClickBank products.

A good article marketing technique for both beginners and advanced involve the application of a repeatable three-part system. This three-part system allows an affiliate to generate massive targeted traffic even if their sales page is not ranked high in the search engines. This article marketing method is without a doubt one of the best system you can use to promote your ClickBank products.

Use Any of the Web 2.0 Sites

There are various web 2.0 sites where you can go to start promoting ClickBank. You can use of any these websites:

- Squidoo
- Blogger
- HubPages

These websites are all very efficient because they rank well in all the search engines.

Use Videos to Promote ClickBank

Another way to advertise ClickBank is to use videos. You know that videos are very popular and they serve as an excellent way to market your ClickBank products. Some individuals prefer watching videos rather than reading the posted articles online. Nowadays, people visit YouTube to find the solutions for any problems they might have. This is why it is an excellent strategy to use in promoting ClickBank.

Promote ClickBank through Email

Once you sign up to become an affiliate with ClickBank, you can start promoting your product using your email. To begin with this technique, you should follow these steps:

- You must sign up for a free affiliate account with ClickBank. All you have to do is to visit the official website of ClickBank and click "sign up". Fill in the online form.
- After signing up, look for products within the marketplace of ClickBank. When you find a good product to promote, click the "promote" button and a hoplink (affiliate link) will be created for you.
- For practice purpose, compose an email to be sent to some of your family members. In your email, you should provide information regarding the product you are promoting then add the link you generated in the previous step. When someone clicks on that link and buys the product, you will certainly get a commission from ClickBank.

Once you get the hang of it and gain some experience you may consider using an auto responder service such as "Aweber" or "Get Response".

Promote ClickBank through Social Media

With millions of internet users across the globe who use social networking sites like Facebook and Twitter, no doubt, social media can help you promote ClickBank. These websites are not just for socializing and entertainment but people use these websites to find products or services that can help them with their problems and needs. Grab this as an opportunity to make money!

5: How to Succeed as an Affiliate

Once you decide to join ClickBank, you have to create your own unique "ID" which is exclusively yours and helps you gain credit for sales made through your marketing efforts. After that, your course of action is going to be something like this.

Find a product

There is an organized directory where vendors display their products in a list. There are thousands of vendors and thousands of products. The products are categorized and organized nicely which makes it easier to navigate through the list. There are certain points to remember while choosing a product.

- Check the price of the product and commission paid for each sale.
- Do not choose a product that has a low commission rate. Make sure the commission rate is 50% or higher. ClickBank deducts a transaction fee from every sale, keep that in mind.
- Choose a niche that you have some knowledge about or have passion for. It would make your work a lot easier and you will receive better results.

- The popularity or gravity is determined by the sales generated and the number of affiliate marketers promoting the product in the last 12 weeks.

- A product low in gravity may also work for you. It is not necessary to aim for the product with the highest gravity. For the most part, there is a lot of competition. Choose something which has not too many sales on record. New ones have a good chance of generating sales.

- Pay a visit to the sales page of the product to make sure that the vendor is doing a good job with the marketing. No point promoting a product which looks good but is a 'turn-down' for customers visiting the sales page.

Affiliate support mechanism

The responsibility of the vendor is not to provide you with a link only. Check the affiliate support system offered by the vendor. Some vendors provide very useful promotional information which comes very handy for an affiliate.
There are sample ads, reviews, endorsements, articles, blogs mailings and signatures which acquaint you to the product. This information is very useful if used as a tool to promote your blogs or reviews.

You should also try to check if there is an affiliate mailing list with the vendor. This list contains details of affiliates and their contact info, which is needed to inform the marketers about the changes in the product or its services. You surely do not want to promote a product for a vendor that changes rules without informing you.

Sign up and promote

When you've checked all the details of the vendor, and you are satisfied, sign up for promoting the respective product. You'll be given a link which is known as a 'hoplink'. It contains your 'Id' along with the vendor's 'Id' and some other details.

Check to see if your hoplink is working by clicking on it. It should take you to the ClickBank order page with your affiliate 'ID' at the bottom. If it does not contain your affiliate 'ID', then your 'ID' has been edited or deleted for some reason, which results in discontinuation. If that is the case, go ahead and create new one.

Cloak your hoplink because a basic hoplink is not protected. There is a chance that a customer will replace your name with their name in the link, and then go ahead with the purchase. They will have a link of their own and the sales would not be done in your name, in which case your commission will be lost.

What does an affiliate marketer want the most? They want the buyers to click the order button and make the purchase, so that they may earn a commission. There are some factors which may deprive you of your rewards.

- The vendors offer multiple payment options, and if ClickBank is not chosen as a medium of purchase, you do not get the credit for sales.
- There is a great 'turn-down" for a potential buyer if there is a long list of unrelated, mixed up list of products. Such a list makes buyers run away because the page is too cumbersome and confusing to them.
- When a buyer tries to reach a site or a product, there are too many links, internal and external, that distract the customer from reaching the actual order page. Most of the times they end up somewhere else, resulting in a wrong sale or no sale at all.

There are some practical issues that you may face when you are a newbie to this sector. You will not be able to withdraw your earnings from ClickBank until several guidelines are met.

- You must have a minimum of five sales

- Sales must be made with two different payment options (visa, MasterCard, PayPal, etc.

It is quite easy to make money on ClickBank if some necessary precautions are taken. Make sure that you are working for a good and competent vendor. There's no point in selling a product that is not worth buying and the vendor that is not worth associating with. With the help of this chapter, you'll be able to recognize and tackle many problems and difficulties.

There are two ways to make money on ClickBank. The first one is to become a vendor. The second option is for those who do not have a digital product to sell at this moment. Instead, you can become an affiliate marketer and try to promote other vendor's product through internet marketing. Yes, it is a marketing job.

What you have to do is to choose a product or a number of products according to your passion or expertise and promote it. There is a huge market out there and people are not aware of the amazing products and services being offered on the internet.

Your job is to capture that market, inform and educate them about the product that you are promoting. You can become an affiliate marketer for any products sold on the internet. You do not have to limit yourself to just ClickBank products.

One of the best ways to promote your product is writing reviews about a certain product or service. If you write an honest review with pros and cons included in your review, people will really appreciate that! They might click on your affiliate link, and you would have earned yourself a commission.

Now remember, the good thing about affiliate marketing is; they don't have to buy the product you are promoting for you to earn a commission. For example: let's say you wrote a review for an iphone 5 and your affiliate link is with amazon. Once they are led to amazon website through your link, you will be credited for any purchases made through your link.

This means you will earn a commission regardless whether the person buys a TV, diamond ring, ipod, piano, clothing, and so on. I'm sure you get the picture. Because this book is about ClickBank affiliate marketing, I can't go into too much detail about other form of affiliate marketing. The information contained in this book should be enough to make you a successful affiliate marketer.

6: How to become a Vendor on ClickBank

To become a vendor on ClickBank, you must have a product to sell. If you believe you have a digital product or service that may attract customers, go ahead and become a vendor. To become a vendor, you have to design a website for yourself, or find a professional to do it for you. This end of ClickBank is very difficult, but the kind of money vendors make, it is worth the effort and hard work.

As we have already discussed earlier, Clickbank functions on the system of selling digital products online. A vendor has the product and he makes use of the platform to attract customers online, spread awareness and sell his products.

However, there are some things you need to do before you can launch your product. You need to have some essential requirements fulfilled in order to make your product visible and presentable. What makes your product presentable? A website that speaks volumes about your product! So remember, the most important part of being a vendor is to have a great website. Here are the 5 steps you need to create a website.

Step 1

Domain name

Think of a domain name. This name will be used as your online address when promoting your digital product. If possible, try to have a catchy name that defines your product.

Another thing to remember is to have a name which is short, so that you can launch it on social media sites, like Twitter, Face Book, YouTube, and other such sites. These sites make it easier to spread the name of your product.

Step 2

Choose a web hosting company

This is the place which houses your website. You start your website under the aegis of a web hosting company that acts as a service provider. There are numerous service providers with dozens of offers. More or less, the services and rates are similar; choose the one that looks pleasing to you.

The hosting company provides you with the space to create your web pages, scripts, email addresses, security, etc. You can install your blogs, forums, and checkout system also.
Hosting companies may confuse you with the plethora of services they offer, the variety is simply overwhelming.

Remember this tip

Choose a plan and hosting that has the cheapest rates, no point wasting money when you have not even started. It is quite easy to upgrade later. When you feel that you are established on the platform and you start making money, go ahead and upgrade your membership. There are dozens of plans available with multiple benefits and facilities.

Choosing an expensive plan in the beginning has no use, as the preparation to create and launch your site may take time and till then you are just wasting money on an expensive subscription.

Step 3

Build your website

This step looks technical but is not as technical. How you build your website depends on the kind of website you want. A simple blog is much easier to set up, however, if you want to have a full fledged website to sell your product, it may take some time to build it.

Do not let this scare you away. You can use WordPress to create many themes automatically. You do not have to be a website developer or know the special codes to do this. You can choose your themes, customize your options, activate plugins and then you're all set.

Step 4

What kind of website do you prefer?

Websites differ in nature because of the function they are designed to perform. Some are ecommerce sites; others are membership or content sites. This kind of difference defines the way your website should be designed. There are instructions and guidelines available on the web hosting platforms about the approach towards your future website.

- Think about considering a niche website. A niche website is a website that is narrow in its coverage. Rather than starting a website for skin care, target your specialization, if you have any, like acne removal, laser treatment, etc. If you want to do something in sports, do not follow a generic pattern of a sports website; try a defined approach, for e.g. football or soccer.

  A well defined website has more chance of capturing audience than a vague one. Know your target audience and then decide on a niche. Once your site is functional, you can monetize it by selling your own products or by carrying endorsements.

- There are two ways of creating websites. One is the Static HTML where the content is loaded and displayed to the public 'as is'. The second is dynamic WordPress. Dynamic indicates that the data is pulled out of the database and displayed category-wise, date-wise, etc. like a blog.

Static HTML sites have lost their charm because you have to learn HTML and even have to buy software like Dreamweaver or Microsoft FrontPage.

The whole website creation was revolutionized by WordPress in 2004. Now, no software has to be bought, all you need to do is to install the WordPress script from your webhost, lunch the admin panel, customize your settings and you are all set.

WordPress is the most dynamic mechanism available for building a website and you can go on increasing the facilities and functions by using plugins. Plugins are scripts that add features to your site and most of them are free. You can install shortcuts and logos for social media sharing, feedback, surveys, and much more. WordPress keeps updating itself with latest features.

Step 5

Be patient!

After having a functional website, you must be wondering as to how long it will take to make sales on your site. This is the most frequently asked question during website creation.

Well, if you have a retail store already, then tell me, did you know how long it was going to take for you to sell 20 pairs of shoes or 100 t-shirts? Of course not!
It is a difficult question to answer. It all depends on how long it takes to get your website noticed, and how soon you are able to market your website accordingly.

With these 5 steps, I hope the fear of creating a website has been alleviated to some extent. Drop your fear and take a plunge. After your website is complete, launch it on ClickBank and see how it gathers attention. If it receives attention, then making money will become easy.

7: Dos and Don'ts for a Vendor

As we have gone through the steps of creating a website, it is time to beware of some mistakes that one is likely to make. These small mistakes may harm you in the long run.

Know your audience first

Do not focus on the money making issue only, your site need to connect with real people. People who are going to buy your product are real people with human emotions. There should be a real connection between your website and the potential buyer. Ask yourself these questions.

- Does your product solve other people problems or generates more competition?
- What kind of persons or group is it going to cater to?
- Why should somebody visit your site rather than visiting an established one?
- Your site should be designed in such a way that it solves the problems of others.

Know the target audience well. If you are catering to a business class section, have a formal approach. If your audience consists of youngsters mostly, follow a casual, laid back approach, they find it easier to connect.

Have some features that your competitors do not have. There should be uniqueness and freshness. Have some refreshing ideas, features that make the visit compelling and leaves users with a good experience. They should have a pleasant memory about visiting your site.

Understand the importance of establishing a bond with your visitors. Mere web pages and good offers won't work in long term. Strike a friendship and make an impact. There are numerous Wikipedia 'like pages' on the net; they won't consider you if you are not unique and you do not deliver more than what you promise.

Forget about building a free website

A free website is not recommended by professionals. First of all, it does not contain your domain name directly, it looks something like this: (sitename.yourwesitename.com). It looks unprofessional and confusing. Your name does not strike to people who are searching for some good products.

The features and facilities of a free website are very limited and the user experience is not so great, and since you will not be ranked high in search engines, you will lose all the traffic.

If you are thinking about changing hosting company, moving from one site to another is an extremely tedious task and most of the time the attempt to move fails due to some technical reasons and your site is lost forever.

To avoid all these headaches, go for a paid webhost and choose a cheap plan.

Avoid generic keywords to attract traffic

How you get ranked in Google is very important. Google ranking are the most unpredictable thing and choosing the right keyword has everything to do with it. Do not choose very generic keywords; go with something narrower, particular. Aim for "long tail keywords", that have been found helpful in generating traffic.

Check profitability of your product or idea

It is very important to know if your digital product or idea has the scope of generating sales. We trust your judgment and opinion about your product but it is always better to get an expert opinion. Do your research and there are dozens of competent advisors on the net who can assist you in choosing and designing a product.

You surely do not want all your efforts and money to get wasted in case the product lacks attractions and utility.

Create your online store

After finishing all this, use the ecommerce plugin provided by WordPress to create your store. There are services like Shopify with multiple services and options for the creation of an online store. Choose the payment setups, like accepting credit cards, bank cards, and PayPal.

Pay attention to details

Use a neat and tidy design for your site. Do not go for flashy colors, loud backgrounds, and bright popup banners all over the page. Simplicity is the new 'thing', it is always beautiful.

Genesis theme on WordPress is the most popular theme with crisp and sharp designs, which are pleasant and user friendly. Highlight the main menu and use sub sections on the menu bar to make the navigation easy. Do not confuse your visitor with dozens of menu options.

Use big font and leave lots of white spaces. It keeps the text light and friendly. Load a version which is accessible on phones and tablets. A site that functions and loads on all devices is the most suitable.

Using a simple website also saves money. Normally website designers charge thousands of dollars to get a website designed, which is useless. Use a one or two column design; it is user friendly and cheap.

After taking these measures and paying attention to these details, now as an owner of a great site, you are all set to sell your product on ClickBank.

If this entire website building and product launch affair is too much for you, hire a programmer or a web designer. There are many out there who are rendering their services and you can choose one according to your needs. They will develop everything from scratch and deliver a functional website for you. It is hassle free and very efficient.

8: Why you should be at Clickbank

Although, we've already mentioned in detail throughout the book why one should choose Clickbank to make money, however, a quick recap will surely help you.

- ClickBank offers a commission rate as high as 75% on some products. Not all products have a similar rate but one is surely going to earn a rate of 50% - 75% in commission fee.
- If you are a vendor, then you can make use of the ads on the ClickBank site and post them on your site or blog. It has been noted that ClickBank ads provide higher profits compared to the ads linked to Google Ad Sense.
- The website also allows the webmasters to integrate the search box in such a way that they connect directly to their site. If a buyer finds something of use or makes a purchase, the commission is added to the affiliate's account.
- No additional qualifications or technical knowledge is needed to become an affiliate of ClickBank. Unlike other marketing jobs that

require a degree or experience, you can go ahead and start selling here right away.

- As an affiliate marketer of ClickBank product, you can go ahead and edit the taglines, Meta tags, descriptions, titles and keywords related to your product. In short, you can get a general idea about a product and then sell it with your own creative ideas or marketing strategies. Creativity is acknowledged and respected here.

- Your personal details are not displayed along with the product that you are selling. This gives you the liberty to promote and sell as many products as you want without being noticed as a mere marketer of goods. This builds faith in customers and makes a reputation.

- A marketer has the choice to promote a broad category of products, or a narrow category for a specific website. You can promote the products in a specific area of expertise, or just a sub category with a small number of products. You can also choose to promote just the keywords, Meta tags or descriptions.

- You can make money by referring your friends and acquaintances to ClickBank. You are rewarded if they join ClickBank under your name.

Let me remind you again, registration for an affiliate account is free on ClickBank. What you need to succeed at ClickBank is willingness to work hard and become an excellent affiliate marketer.

9: 10 Things to know about ClickBank

If you want to succeed at ClickBank, you should try to get to know as much as you can about the subject. As it is believed and advised by wise men, "till you have a complete knowledge about what you are getting yourself into, do not take a plunge." These facts may help you.

1. ClickBank is a third party service provider that links thousands of vendors and marketers through the World Wide Web. It has the latest technology to assist in campaigns and promotional activities. It acts as an intermediary for merchants and affiliates who help sell the products.

2. ClickBank has the world's largest database of affiliates and marketing programs. This gives them the distinction of being the largest affiliate marketplace on the web.

3. This does not mean that the function of ClickBank is limited to being an affiliate marketplace only. It collects commission fees from the merchants and distributes it amongst the affiliates. This ensures transparency in the

system of rewarding the marketers for their hard work. Vendors cannot escape easily.

4. It has a highly advanced tracking system, which too has the distinction of being the best in marketing industry. This makes management of online business very easy.

5. ClickBank has a database of 100,000 affiliates. It is unimaginable to succeed online if these marketers are not available to render services.

6. The registration is an easy process. After becoming a member, you can start selling the product of your choice or multiple products with the same "ClickBank ID". All the promotional banners and details are provided in the company website.

7. We all know that success of a company in long term depends on its honesty and fairness. ClickBank has a fair policy of allotting commission fees to its affiliates, and except for a few exceptional cases of dishonest vendors, normally affiliates are rewarded appropriately.

8. The job of ClickBank is not just to sell products, they also take care of all customer related problems and technical issues, and offer marketing strategies to make your business successful.

9. ClickBank sends a sales report to every vendors. It also sends a paycheck to every affiliate twice a month.

10. ClickBank has over 50,000 products to choose from in all different categories

10: ClickBank is not a Scam

Is ClickBank legitimate or it is a scam? You may be wondering about the legality of this affiliate program. Whoever you are, you have the right to know the truth: ClickBank is not a SCAM. Read on to find why.

Why is ClickBank Not a Scam?

ClickBank is definitely not a scam. It is normal for a person to say that a certain thing is a scam just because he or she does not understand it. You should not think twice to start making money online with ClickBank.

The company guarantees their affiliates that they will be able to get what they expect right from the start. With some effort and patience, you will make sales and earn a commission.

In fact, each product promoted by this program comes with a money back guarantee. A consumer has the right to ask for a refund anytime if they are not satisfied with the product or service. You may request a refund within 60 days of purchase.

If for whatever reason the seller refused to give your money back, all you have to do is contact customer support. They always offer prompt refund.

This is one of the reasons why ClickBank products are among the best-selling items online, giving you a greater chance to make more money.

Having this privilege is certainly a proof that ClickBank is a legitimate company and not a scam. ClickBank is US-based Company that files taxes and complies with all the applicable laws.

Making money with this affiliate program is one of the best ways to make money online. ClickBank will serve as your partner in achieving all your dreams for yourself and for your family.

Conclusion

Throughout the years, ClickBank's mission is to help people maximize their success. Once you are registered, you may utilize the most effective way to sell or promote your products online. Becoming an ClickBank affiliate will be one of the best decisions you will make.

This program will give you the opportunity to make nice passive income every month. How much you make is totally up to you. The more time you invest, more money you will make. Joining the program is free…what else can you ask for?

Hopefully, you have learned a lot by reading this book. Today is the right time for you to make a decision and join ClickBank. You will be glad you did. Unlike other sales platform, ClickBank's digital advertising will empower your profits in ways you never thought possible.

Best of luck to you in your new journey!

www.ingramcontent.com/pod-product-compliance
Lightning Source LLC
Chambersburg PA
CBHW071827170526
45167CB00003B/1451